I0816938

OUR CITIES DEPEND ON US

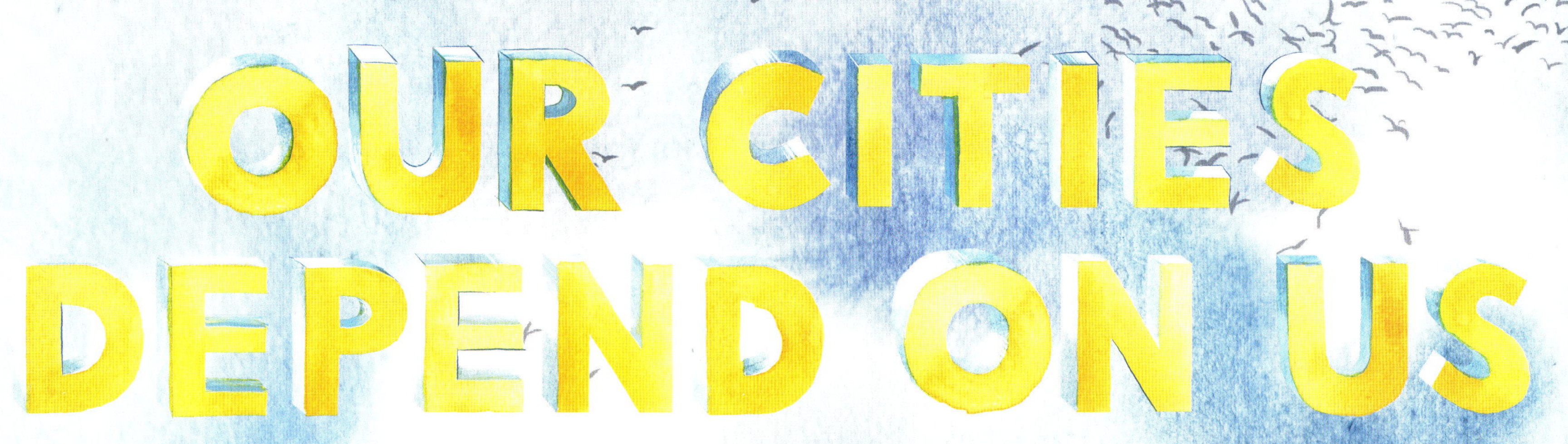

Rethinking Our Urban Areas to Fight Climate Change

Victoria Tentler-Krylov

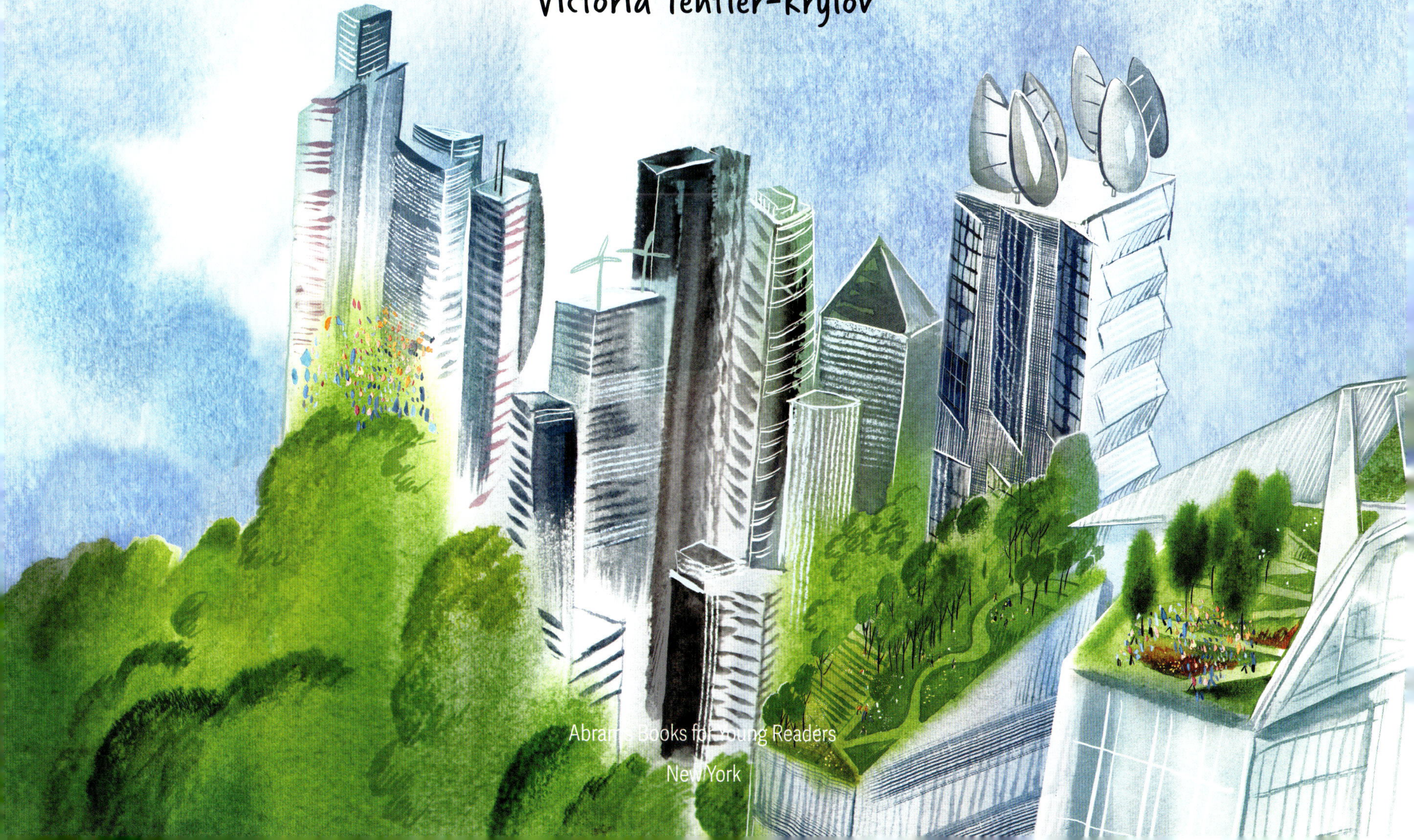

Abrams Books for Young Readers
New York

The air around the Earth—called the atmosphere—acts as a greenhouse.

Have you ever been inside a greenhouse with walls and a roof of glass, where plants and flowers can be grown year-round, no matter the weather? If so, you probably noticed how warm it was, even in winter. That's because the glass traps the sunlight inside.

Our atmosphere wraps around the Earth much like a greenhouse, trapping the Sun's radiation, including heat, and making the planet a comfortable, warm place to live. But because of human activities, our greenhouse has been changing. Carbon dioxide and other gases from factories, power plants, cars, and even farm animals have started to collect in the atmosphere, trapping more heat and making our planet warmer. This is what we mean when we say "global warming."

Global warming is causing many changes in our environment: rising sea levels, droughts, frequent and intense hurricanes and floods, and more. As a result, challenges are being faced by all the living things on our planet: people, animals, even plants.

Our cities need to help fight climate change.

All cities are different, so their challenges are also unique. But every city needs to stay livable, safe, and welcoming to everyone by protecting both its history and its future.

There are so many ideas—big and small.

Just look at how cities are already changing!

SINGAPORE

LIVING ROOFS

The Republic of Singapore

When Earth's temperature rises, cities become even hotter. That's mostly because dark pavement and buildings reflect the Sun's heat back into the air around us.

Trees, grass, and plants help fight climate change: They purify and cool the air and create shade. When there's too much rain, they absorb the water and make flash floods less likely. But it's not easy to find space in a city to plant new trees!

Singaporeans realized building roofs would make wonderful homes for new trees and plants. Now, some call Singapore a capital of green roofs.

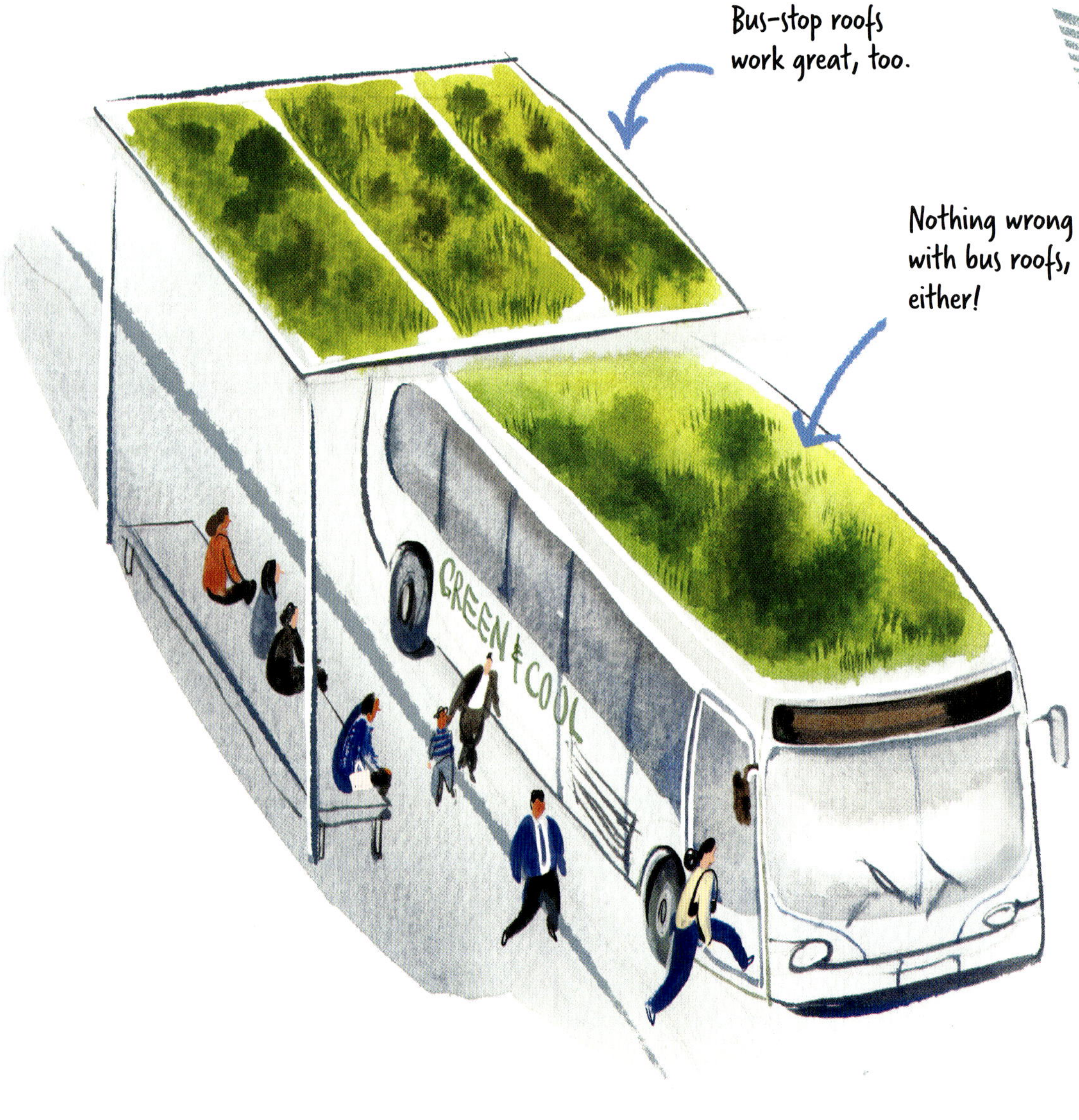

Bus-stop roofs work great, too.

Nothing wrong with bus roofs, either!

NEW YORK

THE BILLION OYSTER PROJECT

Thousands of New York kids participate in the Billion Oyster Project. It's their harbor and their city to protect!

New York, New York, USA

In the early seventeenth century, when Henry Hudson first sailed into the river that would one day take his name, the native Lenape people had already been harvesting oysters in the harbor for thousands of years. Oysters filter particles from the water, improving its quality. When they come together, they form rocklike reefs that provide protection from storms for the surrounding area. By the late nineteenth century, New York had grown, as did New Yorkers' appetite for oysters. But because of overfishing, oysters and their reefs began to disappear, until the last reef was gone in the 1920s.

Now, the Billion Oyster Project is putting the oysters back so they can form reefs again, protect the city from water surges, and help clean the water.

MILAN
VERTICAL FOREST

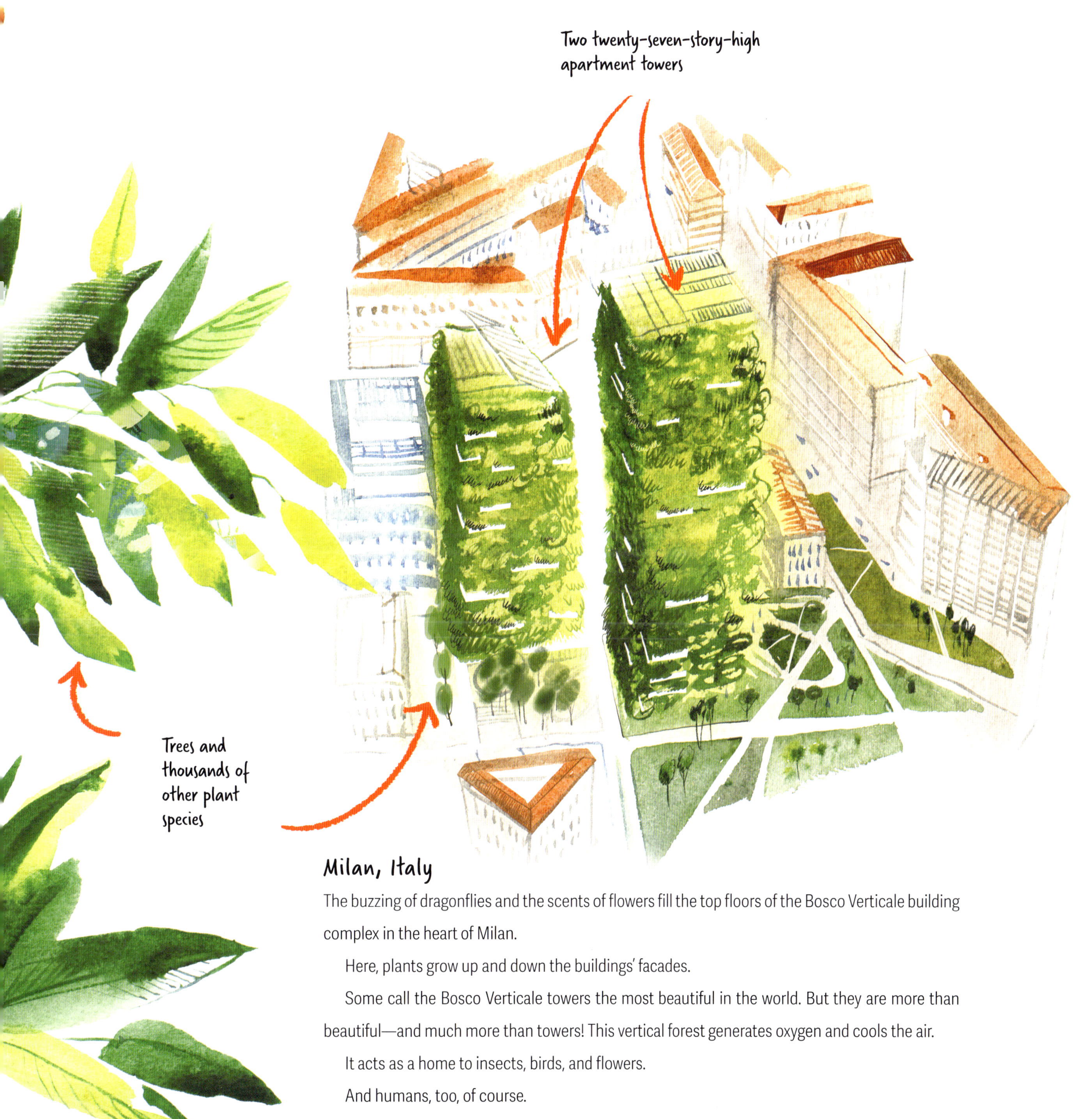

Milan, Italy

The buzzing of dragonflies and the scents of flowers fill the top floors of the Bosco Verticale building complex in the heart of Milan.

Here, plants grow up and down the buildings' facades.

Some call the Bosco Verticale towers the most beautiful in the world. But they are more than beautiful—and much more than towers! This vertical forest generates oxygen and cools the air.

It acts as a home to insects, birds, and flowers.

And humans, too, of course.

CHICAGO

REINVENTING THE CHICAGO RIVER

Chicago, Illinois, USA

Years ago, steel mills, lumberyards, and soap factories that lined the Chicago River dumped toxic chemicals into its waters. People stayed away. So did fish, birds, and most marine plants.

In the 1970s, Chicagoans began to clean and improve the river. The work of clearing trash, lining the shores with trees, and protecting the water is ongoing, but now the river is Chicagoans' treasure.

Keeping the water healthy makes life so much better for humans! The same is true for animal species that call the river home; now they have a place to play, nest, and shelter in it during storms and floods.

CHICAGO RIVER

ROSARIO

CITY FARMS

Rosario, Argentina

The best climate change–fighting projects achieve more than just one goal, and the city of Rosario may take the prize in doing the most with its urban farms.

New farms are being built in abandoned parking lots and open spaces.

The farmlands absorb rainwater, reducing the risk of both flooding and wildfires. They act as homes to thousands of plant and animal species. Of course, they also make the city more beautiful. And because there's no longer a need to bring vegetables to the city from elsewhere, there are fewer trucks on the roads. This means cleaner air and less traffic!

Rosario's citizens decide what to grow! And if there is more than they need, they can sell the extra produce or share with their neighbors.

VENICE

MOSE

(Modulo Sperimentale Elettromeccanico/Experimental Electromechanical Module)

Venice, Italy

A unique and ancient city, Venice is built on hundreds of small islands scattered around the Venetian Lagoon in the Adriatic Sea. The lagoon both protected Venice and threatened it with storms and floods. Venice has been slowly sinking for centuries; and sea-level rise makes the problem worse. To save their city, Venetians built seventy-eight giant, movable gates that block the Adriatic Sea tides from entering the lagoon.

The MOSE gates use seawater to operate. Not everyone agrees about the project: Many worry about the health of the lagoon sea life or how long the construction is taking. It's still not done!

But now, Venice has a future.

When the weather is clear, the gates, filled with water, lie on the seabed.
Before a storm, air is pumped into the gate, displacing the water.
The gates rise, stopping the waves.
After the storm, water returns and fills the gates, which lower to the seabed.
In wet weather, the city installs raised sidewalks to keep people from wading through the rising water.

BANGKOK

CENTENARY PARK

Bangkok, Thailand

As in many cities around the world, flooding in Bangkok is becoming worse with climate change. What to do with all the water?

Centenary Park is designed so the sloping lawn diverts the floods away from the surrounding streets.

Rainwater runs toward a retention pond. There, water waits for the dry season, when it will be used to nourish plants and flowers.

Central London
River Flow
Tidal flow from
the North Sea

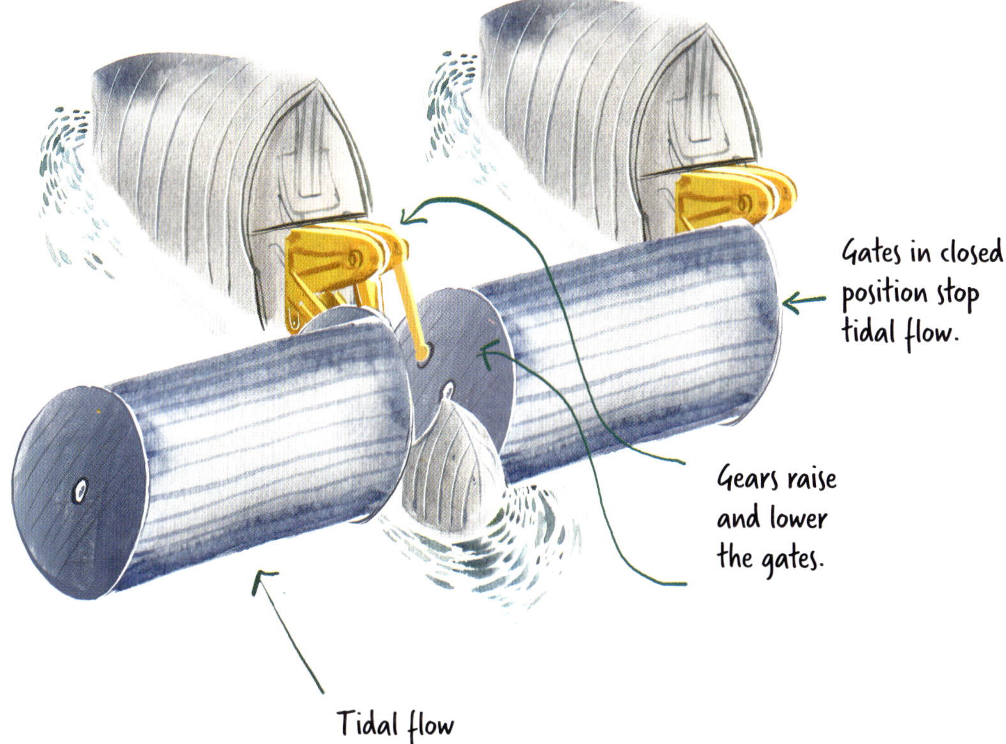

LONDON

THE THAMES BARRIER

London, England

The city of London is miles away from the coast. Still, for centuries, storm surges and rising tides on the North Sea have caused flooding along the banks of the River Thames, which snakes through the city toward the sea. In the twentieth century, Londoners decided to build a barrier to act as a temporary dam to block the river and head off the tides from reaching central London.

The Thames Barrier is made up of several circular rotating gates. If the river isn't likely to flood, the gates are filled with water, so they are submerged. However, if flooding is anticipated, the gates empty of water. This makes them rotate up to the surface.

The barrier is used several times a year, but scientists predict it will happen a lot more often as sea levels continue to rise. Engineers are already designing updates to the barrier: When finished, it will protect London from floods for years to come.

UGANDA

KYABIRWA SURGICAL CENTER

Jinja, Uganda

Almost three-quarters of Uganda's population lives in rural areas. When they get sick, they must travel hours to get to the closest hospital. And if there is a flood or a drought, the journey becomes even harder.

Kyabirwa is the first clinic of its kind in Africa. It brings state-of-the-art technology to the area and is also built to help fight climate change. This means it will keep local families healthy for many years to come. Not only that, it is also designed as a model, so that other rural or remote communities around the world can learn from the way Kyabirwa was built and how it operates.

Perforated, or holed, walls allow natural ventilation to keep the building cool.
Red clay, dug from the area surrounding the clinic, was used to make the tiles and bricks.

MELBOURNE

THE GREEN LANEWAYS

Melbourne, Australia

With almost 5 million people living in close proximity, Melbourne, one of the largest cities in Australia, struggles with crowds, heat, and air pollution. It needs to become cooler, shadier, and more livable.

In a word, it needs to be greener.

Melbourne's famous laneways—narrow alleys that split city blocks—are already filled with street art, shops, and cafés. Now, the city is helping the neighbors plant trees, flowers, and grasses wherever they can fit them. The cooler, quieter, greener laneways fill with people even during the hottest months.

CAF

ROTTERDAM

FLOATING PARK MADE OF RECYCLED LITTER

Rotterdam, the Netherlands

Rotterdam's canals flow out into the North Sea, so every ice-cream spoon and plastic cup thrown into the water eventually ends up in the Atlantic Ocean. Catching all the trash before it reaches the ocean prevents it from harming sea animals. But what to do with it? Rotterdam residents realized it could be used as foundations for a new floating park!

The plastic is compacted into interlocking floating blocks.

In 2018, the first park was built. As Rotterdam's residents work to reduce the use of plastic, they also collect most of the canal trash in floating traps to be used for future parks. Other cities are already inspired to convert their own plastic waste into welcoming habitats for humans and animals.

Windows
Plywood
Doors
Pipes

PORTLAND

BUILDING WITH REUSED MATERIALS

Portland, Oregon, USA

Nomadic peoples of the past often took apart their homes to bring them to a new place. Some still live this way—and in Portland, builders followed their cue. Old houses and office buildings are carefully taken apart instead of being destroyed. Beams, doors, bricks, and many other building parts are reused in new homes. This saves energy that would have otherwise been spent making new materials and bringing them to Portland!

But how are the new buildings in Portland built? With the future in mind. When the time comes, they can be easily taken apart so the old materials can begin a new life as part of a new building.

VANCOUVER

TIMBER SKYSCRAPERS

Vancouver, Canada

Materials for Canadian skyscrapers often used to come from hundreds or thousands of miles away. The huge ships and trucks that carried them were bad for the environment. Using local materials is much better, and in heavily forested Canada, this means wood!

Wood has been used to build homes since ancient times. But it has always been thought of as risky, fire-prone, and too unstable for tall buildings. The future is here for timber skyscrapers! Even better, the wood comes from managed forests. This way, old trees are protected, and new ones are planted to replace those that are cut down.

Cross-laminated timber

New wood products called "mass timber" are much stronger and safer than regular wood. This makes them great for construction of tall buildings! One type of a mass timber product is "cross-laminated timber." It involves gluing overlapping strips of wood together under extreme pressure to form superstrong panels.

AUTHOR'S NOTE

What do you think your city will look like when you grow up? How will it change? And what will be your part in its transformation?

This book grew out of my passion for the Italian city of Venice and its magic. I fell in love with Venice as an architecture student and returned to the city every few years since. Later, when I became an architect in the early aughts, I learned about the concept of "green building": designing and building in such a way that reduces the impact on the environment, both from the construction and from use. Architects were starting to take action against climate change!

In the meantime, floods that threatened Venice got worse, and I began to wonder whether my kids would ever get to see the city before it was lost to the sea. I didn't realize that work on MOSE, the underwater flood barriers now protecting the Venetian Lagoon, had already started. But other cities all over the world were also wondering about their futures. Not every city could build complicated systems like MOSE. Climate change is bringing about unpredictable weather, floods, droughts, and storms. In turn, this is creating more poverty and injustice in places that are already struggling.

Can cities be rethought to not only fight climate change, but to become more sustainable, fair, and welcoming to everyone? Every city is different. It is shaped by the culture, history, and nature of its place and its people. As more and more cities plan for their futures in the face of climate change, they have much to teach each other. We also have to be fair and help each other. This means that those countries and companies that contribute to climate change the most should take responsibility for it and support those that need help.

You are probably already taking climate action. You recycle, protect and respect nature, and try to reduce your use of energy. But that's not all you can do. You can learn about careers that focus on greening the planet. You can make your voice heard by your local government. Most importantly, you can come up with new ideas and share them with others.

Because our cities depend on all of us to make those ideas reality.

CHECK OUT THESE WEBSITES TO LEARN MORE ABOUT CLIMATE ACTION:

kids.earth.org/life-on-land/how-can-we-build-a-sustainable-city-a-kid-friendly-guide/

climatekids.nasa.gov/kids-guide-to-climate-change/

amnh.org/explore/ology/climate-change

SELECT BIBLIOGRAPHY

Cohen, Steven. *The Sustainable City.* New York: Columbia University Press, 2017.

Joachim, Mitchell. *The New City: How to Build Our Sustainable Urban Future.* New York: Columbia University Press, 2023.

Wheeler, Stephen, and Christina Rosan. *Reimagining Sustainable Cities: Strategies for Designing Greener, Healthier, More Equitable Communities.* Oakland: University of California Press, 2021.

Singapore, the Republic of Singapore: Living Roofs

Baile, Stephanie. "Green roofs are sprouting up on buses." *CNN*, June 18, 2019. https://www.cnn.com/2019/06/03/health/green-roofs-singapore-buses-intl/index.html.

Relman, Eliza. "Why so many buildings in Singapore are covered in plants." *Business Insider*, September 19, 2023. https://www.businessinsider.com/why-buildings-in-singapore-covered-in-plants-government-incentives-2023-9.

New York, New York, USA: The Billion Oyster Project

"Billion Oyster Project," Billion Oyster Project, https://www.billionoysterproject.org.

Milan, Italy: Bosco Verticale (Vertical Forest)

"Bosco Veritcale / Boeri Studio," ArchDaily, November 23, 2015, https://www.archdaily.com/777498/bosco-verticale-stefano-boeri-architetti.

"Vertical Forest Milan," Stefano Boeri Architetti, https://www.stefanoboeriarchitetti.net/en/project/vertical-forest/.

Chicago, Illinois, USA: Reinventing the Chicago River

"Get Involved," Friends of the Chicago River, https://www.chicagoriver.org/get-involved/volunteer/chicago-river-day.

Rosario, Argentina: City Farms

Avampato, Christa. "Urban ecology that saved Argentina's Rosario held up as a model for others." *Mongabay*, December 31, 2021, https://news.mongabay.com/2021/12/urban-ecology-that-saved-argentinas-rosario-held-up-as-a-model-for-others/.

Venice, Italy: MOSE (Modulo Sperimentale Elettromeccanico/ Experimental Electromechanical Module)

Harvan, Chico, and Stefano Pitrelli. "An engineering marvel just saved Venice from a flood. What about when seas rise?" *Washington Post*, November 27, 2022. https://www.washingtonpost.com/climate-solutions/2022/11/26/venice-floods-mose-barrier-climate/.

Keahey, John. *Venice Against the Sea – A City Besieged.* New York: Thomas Dunne Books / St. Martins Press, 2002.

"Per la difesa di Venezia e della laguna dalle acque alte," Consorzio Venezia Nuova, Ministero delle Infrastrutture e dei Trasporti. https://mosevenezia.eu.

Phelan, Joseph. "Italy's plan to save Venice from sinking." *BBC*, September 27, 2022. https://www.bbc.com/future/article/20220927-italys-plan-to-save-venice-from-sinking.

Silvestri, Manuel, and Federico Maccioni. "Venice kept dry as dam system wards off exceptional high tide." *Reuters*, November 22, 2022. https://www.reuters.com/world/europe/venice-kept-dry-dam-system-wards-off-exceptional-high-tide-2022-11-22/.

Viviano, Frank. "Saving Venice from flooding may destroy the ecosystem that sustains it." *National Geographic*, July 25, 2022. https://www.nationalgeographic.com/environment/article/saving-venice-from-flooding-may-destroy-the-ecosystem-that-sustains-it.

Bangkok, Thailand: Centenary Park

Holmes, Damian. "Chulalongkorn University Centenary Park – green infrastructure for the city of Bangkok." *World Landscape Architect*, April 19, 2019. https://worldlandscapearchitect.com/chulalongkorn-centenary-park-green-infrastructure-for-the-city-of-bangkok/?v=7516fd43adaa.

London, England: The Thames Barrier

"The Thames Barrier," 21st Century Challengers, Royal Geographical Society. https://21stcenturychallenges.org/the-thames-barrier/.

Jinja, Uganda: Kyabirwa Surgical Center

"Kyabirwa Surgical Center," Global Surgical Initiatives, Inc. https://www.kyabirwasc.org.

"Mount Sinai Kyabirwa Uganda Surgical Facility," Perkins-Eastman. https://perkinseastman.com/projects/mount-sinai-kyabirwa-uganda-surgical-facility/.

Melbourne, Australia: The Green Laneways

"Greening laneways," City of Melbourne. https://www.melbourne.vic.gov.au/community/greening-the-city/green-infrastructure/Pages/greening-laneways.aspx.

Rotterdam, the Netherlands: Floating Park Made of Recycled Litter

Lekka Angelopoulou, Sofia. "Rotterdam's floating park is made entirely from recycled plastic waste found in the Maas River." *DesignBoom*, July 13, 2018. https://www.designboom.com/design/rotterdam-floating-park-recycled-plastic-waste-river-07-13-2018/.

Portland, Oregon, USA: Building with Reused Materials

"Deconstruction permit requirements," City of Portland, Oregon. https://www.portland.gov/bps/climate-action/decon/deconstruction-requirements#:~:text=All%20single%2Ddwelling%20structures%20(houses,delay%20provisions%20of%20Title%2033.

Vancouver, Canada: Timber Skyscrapers

Kergin, Brendan. "Here's a look at the epic mass timber building set to tower over Mount Pleasant." *Vancouver Is Awesome*, October 20, 2022. https://www.vancouverisawesome.com/local-news/renderings-mass-timber-tower-mount-pleasant-vancouver-5980411.

*To Professor Ricardo Scofidio, a brilliant architect,
mastermind of the High Line,
and a lifelong influence on me and many others.
Thank you for everything you taught us.*

The art for this book was created with traditional watercolor and Procreate software.

Cataloging-in-Publication Data has been applied for and
may be obtained from the Library of Congress.

ISBN 978-1-4197-5669-6
eISBN 978-1-64700-402-6

Edited by Howard W. Reeves
Book design by Heather Kelly

Printed and bound in China
10 9 8 7 6 5 4 3 2 1

ABRAMS is represented in the UK and Europe by Abrams & Chronicle Books, 1 West Smithfield,
London EC1A 9JU and Média-Participations, 57 rue Gaston Tessier, 75166 Paris, France.
abramsandchronicle.co.uk and media-participations.com
info@abramsandchronicle.co.uk

ABRAMS The Art of Books
195 Broadway, New York, NY 10007
abramsbooks.com